CONTENTS

Dream Diary

Recall your dreams by:
- Describing people or animals you saw
- Noting sounds you heard
- Mapping out places you went

Take Your Dreams Further

Think about the people, animals, or objects in one of your dreams.
Write about what you think happened to them after you woke up.

_____

_____

_____

_____

_____

_____

_____

_____

_____

_____

_____

                                      _____

                                      _____

                                      _____

                                      _____

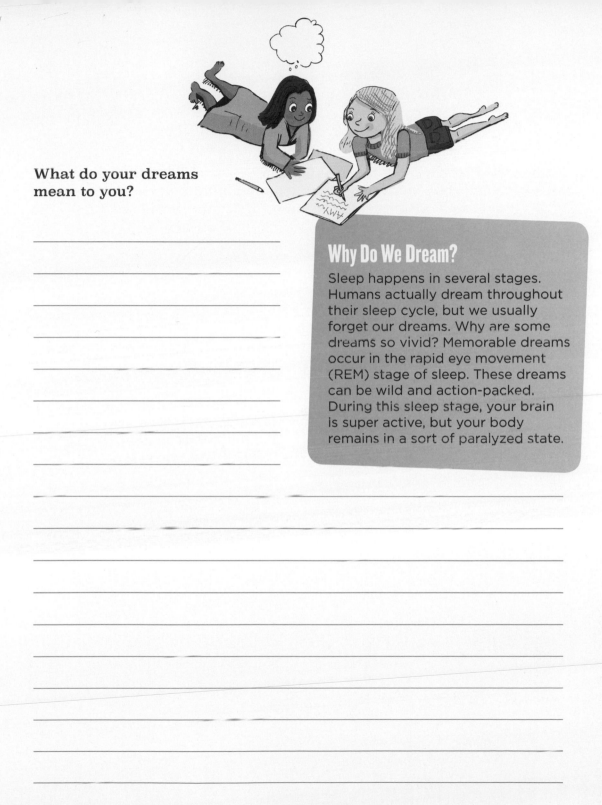

What do your dreams mean to you?

_____

_____

_____

_____

_____

_____

_____

Why Do We Dream?

Sleep happens in several stages. Humans actually dream throughout their sleep cycle, but we usually forget our dreams. Why are some dreams so vivid? Memorable dreams occur in the rapid eye movement (REM) stage of sleep. These dreams can be wild and action-packed. During this sleep stage, your brain is super active, but your body remains in a sort of paralyzed state.

_____

_____

_____

_____

_____

_____

_____

Making a Difference

Kids have a lot of power to make a difference in the world. Use this space to write a few sentences about what kind of change you'd like to be a part of in your community or the world.

_____

_____

_____

_____

_____

_____

_____

_____

_____

_____

_____

_____

_____

_____

Think of something kind you could
do for a friend, family member, or
neighbor. What would that be?

_____

_____

_____

_____

_____

_____

_____

_____

_____

_____

_____

_____

_____

Train Tracks

You finally embark on a long-awaited train ride. Write the beginning of a story about where you're going, what you see, and what problems pop up along the way.

Ask a sibling or friend to take over "conducting" the story and write the second half of the story here. You may be surprised where your story ends up!

_____

_____

_____

_____

_____

_____

_____

_____

_____

_____

_____

_____

_____

_____

_____

Tip!
Consider sharing your writing with others. Feedback can help improve your writing.

Brave

Complete this crisscross puzzle full of words related to bravery.

4 Letters
BOLD
GAME

5 Letters
NERVY
NOBLE

6 Letters
CHEEKY
DARING
GRITTY
HEROIC
SPUNKY
PLUCKY

7 Letters
DASHING
DEFIANT
VALIANT

8 Letters
FEARLESS
INTREPID
RESOLUTE
SPIRITED
UNAFRAID

9 Letters
AUDACIOUS
CONFIDENT
DAUNTLESS
STEADFAST
TENACIOUS

10 Letters
COURAGEOUS
DETERMINED
HEADSTRONG
PERSISTENT

11 Letters
ADVENTUROUS
INDOMITABLE
LIONHEARTED
UNFLINCHING

12 Letters
HIGH-SPIRITED

Write about a time you overcame a challenge.

_____

_____

_____

_____

_____

_____

_____

_____

_____

_____

BOLD

Write the name of your favorite insect or animal in the circle. On each line, write a cool fact about it.

_____

_____

_____

_____

Quick Challenges
ANIMALS

Write the first three lines of a story about a bird that loves to sing.

_____

_____

_____

_____

Find a quiet place. Close your eyes and breathe deeply. Imagine you're staring into fog and an animal appears. Open your eyes and write about what you see and feel.

_____

_____

_____

_____

You're a wildlife biologist studying polar bears in the Arctic.
Write a few notes about your day.

_____

_____

_____

_____

Write a conversation you'd like to have with your
pet. If you don't have one, imagine a conversation
between you and your dream pet.

_____

_____

_____

_____

What are your favorite things about some of your favorite animals? Write
them down here, then again in colorful chalk on your sidewalk or driveway.

_____

_____

_____

_____

Dolphin Speak

You've just discovered how to communicate with wild dolphins!
Write down what you'd like to ask them. What do you think
they would have to say?

You're giving a speech about your breakthrough. What was your experience like when you talked to the dolphins?

_____

_____

_____

_____

_____

_____

_____

_____

_____

_____

_____

_____

_____

_____

_____

Food Fight

A hungry leopard is chasing a capybara through the Amazon rainforest. Imagine you're a sportscaster and write your play-by-play commentary on the action below.

Write a story from the capybara's
point of view.

_____

_____

_____

_____

_____

_____

_____

_____

_____

_____

_____

_____

_____

_____

_____

_____

_____

_____

Animal Rescue!

Imagine you and a friend have started an animal rescue. Write a blog post about who you are and what your organization will do.

Meet the Animals

Write about the animals in your care.
Include a photo or drawing of each one.

Pet Detective

Write about a pet detective on the trail of a lost cat. What clues do you follow? How do you know where to look? What happens when you find the cat?

_____

_____

_____

_____

_____

_____

_____

_____

_____

_____

_____

_____

LOST CAT

Write up a poster about the missing cat.

Name: _____

Looks like: _____

_____

_____

_____

Last seen: _____

_____

_____

_____

Favorite treats: _____

_____

_____

_____

_____

Hero Animals

Write a news story about a heroic animal. For example, you could feature a search and rescue dog who found a lost child or a cat who alerted its owner to a house fire.

The Who, What, When, and Where

Start your news story with an outline. Make notes about where and when the rescue happened and who was involved. Create quotes from witnesses to highlight important details. End with a summary.

Introduction

_____

_____

_____

_____

_____

Body of Story

_____

_____

_____

_____

Conclusion

_____

_____

_____

_____

The community honors the heroic animal with
an award. What is the animal's acceptance speech?

Plan a Nonfiction Book

Think about a wild animal you love and want to know more about. Find out more and write down interesting things you discover about it.

Check Your Sources

Use reliable sources when writing factual information. A good source is:
• Current
• Written by a respected author
• Accurate

How will you start your book? You could begin with what inspired you to write it and what you hope readers will learn from it.

_____

_____

_____

_____

_____

_____

_____

_____

_____

_____

_____

_____

_____

_____

_____

_____

_____

Tip!
To make sure a fact is accurate, verify it with a different reliable source.

Animal Cam

Ask an adult for help finding and watching a live animal cam, such as one that watches a bald eagle's nest. Write about the animal's behaviors and activities.

Life can be hard for wild animals. Read about the wild animal you're watching. What are some difficulties they have overcome? How can humans help?

_____

_____

_____

_____

_____

_____

_____

_____

_____

_____

_____

_____

_____

_____

_____

Write a Sympathy Note

When someone you know has a family member or a pet pass away, a sympathy note lets them know you care.

Explain why you are writing.

If you have a nice memory or two of the person or pet who died, you can mention them.

Tell your friend you are sorry for their loss.

It's more personal to handwrite this kind of letter.

Dear XXXXX,

I heard the sad news about your XXXXXXX. I am very sorry for your family's loss. Your XXXXX was a very nice person. If you want to talk about her sometime, I am happy to listen.

Your friend,
XXXX

Offer to listen to your friend if they want to talk about their loss.

Handwrite the first draft of your note here.

_____

_____

_____

_____

_____

_____

_____

_____

_____

_____

_____

_____

_____

_____

_____

Tip!
Write your final note on nice paper or a card.

Metamorphosis

Color this illustration. Can you find 14 hidden objects in the picture?

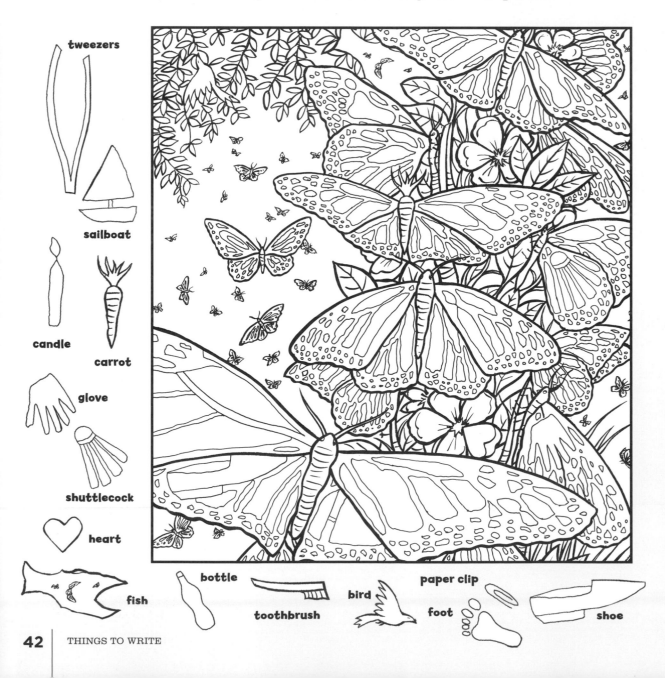

tweezers

sailboat

candle

carrot

glove

shuttlecock

heart

fish

bottle

toothbrush

bird

paper clip

foot

shoe

Metamorphosis is a process of transformation.
A butterfly starts as a caterpillar. Write about what it would
be like to move into a cocoon and then emerge as a butterfly.

What's the first thing you see when you wake up in the morning?

_____

_____

_____

_____

Find an object in your house. What does it look like, what does it do, and where did it come from?

_____

_____

_____

_____

Imagine that an amazing new food truck came to your neighborhood. Write a raving review as if you're a customer.

_____

_____

_____

_____

Your new neighbors have some weird habits. You find out they're aliens from another planet. How do you become friends despite your differences?

_____

_____

_____

_____

Notice the street signs in your neighborhood. Reimagine the names of the streets to better describe the area (Main Street might now be "Green Trees Street" or "Friend's House Street").

_____

_____

_____

_____

Write a list of your top 10 weird and favorite facts about the place where you live.

1. _____
2. _____
3. _____
4. _____
5. _____
6. _____
7. _____
8. _____
9. _____
10. _____

Go Back in Time

You have the power to travel back in time to a famous moment in history. What event do you choose? Write about the experience. What did you wear, eat, say, or do?

It's time to head back to the present! How do you get back to your timeline?

_____

_____

_____

_____

_____

_____

_____

_____

_____

_____

_____

_____

_____

_____

_____

_____

_____

A World of Color

What colors do you see when you look out your window? If you could change the colors of the things you see outside, such as the trees or your street, what colors would you make them? Write about this crazy new colorful world.

_____

_____

_____

_____

_____

_____

_____

_____

_____

_____

_____

_____

_____

Write about a character experiencing seasons for the first time. Try using colorful language to describe what your character sees as the seasons change.

Rainy Day

It's raining! It's pouring! Find at least 12 differences between these pictures.

On a rainy day, you discover a magic umbrella. Using words from the differences you found in the pictures, write about your umbrella. What does it look like? What powers does it have? Where will it take you?

Neighborhood Notes

Interview an older person in your neighborhood or community who grew up there. Make a list of questions, such as "How was the neighborhood different when you were growing up?" If you can't find a person to interview, imagine who you would interview in your neighborhood or community. Ask an adult for permission before you interview someone.

Go back in time! What do you think it would have been like to be a kid in your neighborhood 50 years ago?

_____

_____

_____

_____

_____

_____

_____

_____

_____

_____

_____

_____

_____

_____

Helpful Questions

Open-ended questions encourage people to think and share. When interviewing someone, follow your curiosity. Ask questions about details. Avoid questions that can be answered with "yes" or "no."

Parade Day

You're a town official planning an annual parade, but things go terribly wrong. Write about the inspiration for your parade, what went wrong, and the zany outcome.

_____

_____

_____

_____

_____

_____

_____

_____

_____

_____

_____

_____

_____

_____

_____

Alien Visitors

Write about an alien trying to land a spaceship somewhere on Earth. How will they decide where to land? What will they find when they touch down?

_____

_____

_____

_____

_____

_____

_____

_____

_____

_____

_____

_____

_____

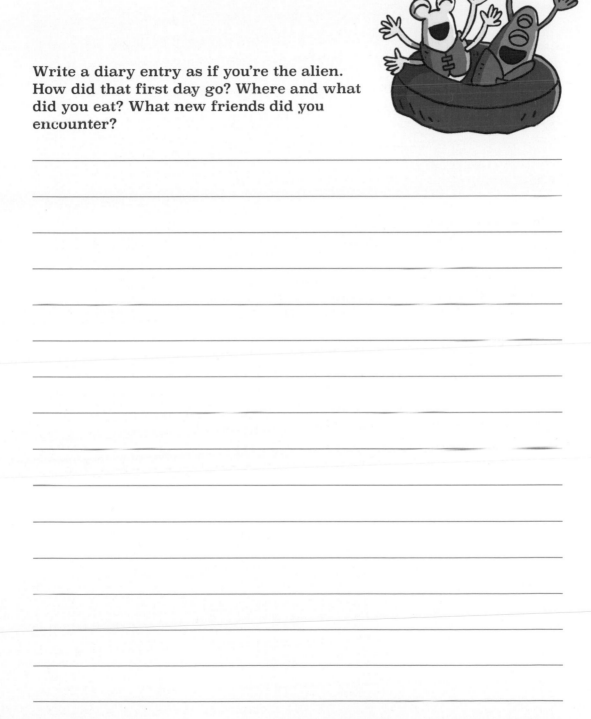

Write a diary entry as if you're the alien. How did that first day go? Where and what did you eat? What new friends did you encounter?

_____

_____

_____

_____

_____

_____

_____

_____

_____

_____

_____

_____

_____

Start a Neighborhood Newsletter

What kind of stories would you include? Perhaps a neighbor just built a cool, new tree house or got a puppy. Is there anyone you can invite to share their news or stories for your newsletter?

_____

_____

_____

_____

_____

_____

_____

_____

_____

_____

_____

_____

_____

_____

Draft a story that takes place where you live and include it in the first issue of your newsletter.

_____

_____

_____

_____

_____

_____

_____

_____

_____

_____

_____

_____

_____

_____

_____

Shout-Out

Make a list of people in your community who work hard or solve problems. Who do you most admire? Perhaps it's a dedicated postal worker, bus driver, or teacher.

Saying Thanks

Write a letter to the editor of a local newspaper praising this person. Share information about:

- Why you feel strongly about this person's contributions
- What these contributions are, or what problems this person is working to solve
- Why others should care

Spreading Love

Draft some postcards to friends or relatives. If you're wondering what to include, try telling them a bit about your daily life. You can also include questions and ask that they write you back. Ask an adult for help finding postcards, addresses, and stamps, and then put your postcards in the mail.

Dear Alex,

How are you? My summer is great, but I'm super bored today. I could have texted you, but a postcard seemed more special. Plus, it takes more time to write!

I miss talking and joking around with you. Remember the skateboards we made for Horatio Hamster? I hope we can see each other soon.

Your friend,
Ava

P.S. Write me back!

Alex Smith
75 Willow Street
Flisk, MT 55562

POST CARD

POST CARD

Welcome to Chillville

Find your way from START to FINISH. Watch out for one way streets and other vehicles!

As you make your way through town, see how many things you can find that rhyme with *chill*. Imagine what it's like to live in Chillville.

_____

_____

_____

_____

_____

_____

_____

_____

_____

_____

_____

_____

_____

_____

_____

_____

_____

Go for a walk and write about what you see.

_____

_____

_____

_____

You're standing at the edge of the biggest waterfall in the world. Jot down phrases about what it feels like, such as *hair whipping in wind, misty spray, or stand back!*

_____

_____

_____

_____

You find a talking tree. What does it say about the view?

_____

_____

_____

_____

Create the beginning of a ghost story to tell around a campfire.

_____

_____

_____

_____

You wake up on a deserted island full of ancient statues that can talk. What is a piece of advice the statues give you to survive living outdoors?

_____

_____

_____

_____

You slip on a pair of enchanted hiking boots that can walk on air. What happens as you hike up into the clouds?

_____

_____

_____

_____

Pop Quiz

Create a nature quiz to stump your friends.

Write your answer key here.

Volcanic Adventure

While camping, you wake up to find you're on a volcano that's about to erupt. The sneakers you left outside have started to melt. Write about what happens next.

_____

_____

_____

_____

_____

_____

_____

_____

_____

_____

_____

_____

_____

_____

_____

_____

_____

_____

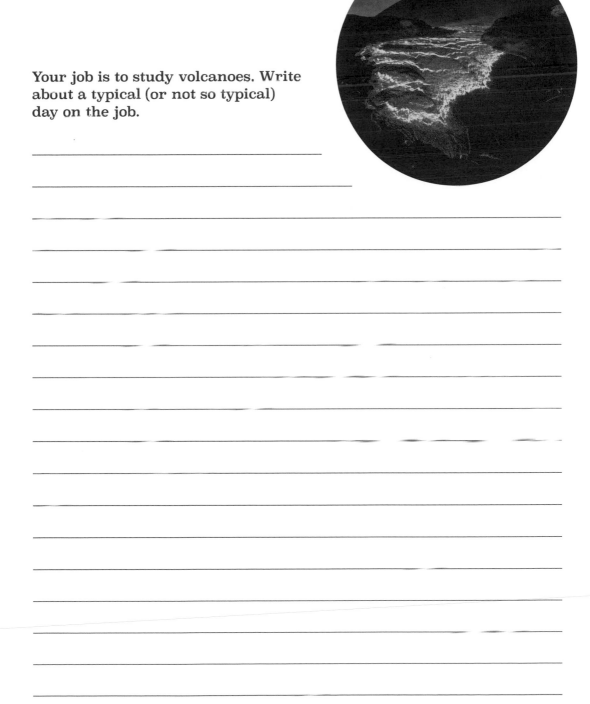

Your job is to study volcanoes. Write about a typical (or not so typical) day on the job.

_____

_____

_____

_____

_____

_____

_____

_____

_____

_____

_____

_____

_____

_____

_____

_____

Summer Storm Story

Write a short story that takes place during a summer thunderstorm. Use descriptive words to describe the sounds of the storm and the feelings of the characters.

Write another story about the same storm,
but from the point of view of a frog.

_____

_____

_____

_____

_____

_____

_____

_____

_____

_____

_____

_____

_____

_____

_____

Colorful Seasons

Use different-colored crayons, pencils, or markers to write words or phrases about the outdoors. Match colors to words, such as writing *grass* in green and *ice* in silver. Then mix things up!

ICE

grass

Tremendous Tree House

You wake up in a fantasy tree house. Use strong verbs to describe what happens next.

_____

_____

_____

_____

_____

_____

_____

_____

_____

_____

_____

_____

_____

Strong Verbs

Powerful verbs can charge up your writing. They help the reader better understand what you're trying to communicate. For example, did a bird *move*, or did it *fly, flap,* or *zoom*? Did you *go* from one end of the tree house to the other, or did you *tiptoe, leap,* or *race*?

Create a timeline that shows what happened that day and when.

1

_____
_____
_____

2

_____
_____
_____

3

_____
_____
_____

4

_____
_____
_____

5

_____
_____
_____

Wild Wordplay

Write sentences with outdoor-related words and words that sound the same but have different meanings (like *bear* and *bare* or *flower* and *flour*).

You've landed a small plane in the middle of the wilderness—there's no one around for hundreds of miles. Using as many words as you can from your list, write a story about where you land and what happens when you get out of the plane to explore.

_____

_____

_____

_____

_____

_____

_____

_____

_____

_____

_____

_____

_____

_____

Homonyms

Homonyms are words that sound the same but have different meanings. Such as *meat* and *meet*. Homonyms can also have the same spelling but different meanings—for instance, the words *bat* and *fair* have multiple meanings.

Autumn Leaves

You're a leaf falling from a tree. Write about your life. How did you grow, and what will you do next?

_____

_____

_____

_____

_____

_____

_____

_____

_____

_____

_____

_____

_____

_____

_____

_____

_____

Write a letter to a neighbor and offer to rake leaves. Tell them about yourself and why you like to spend time outdoors. Ask an adult to help you deliver it.

Places to Go

Write about what it's like to be a river or a mountain. What surprising things happen? What changes during a few months or a thousand years?

Imagine climbing the world's tallest peak.
What happens on your journey to the top?

Ocean Find

The names of 16 ocean animals are hidden in the letters below. Some names are across. Others are up and down. Find the rest!

Word List

CLAM
CRAB
~~DOLPHIN~~
JELLYFISH
LOBSTER
OCTOPUS
SEAHORSE
SEAL
SHARK
SQUID
STARFISH
STINGRAY
SWORDFISH
TURTLE
WALRUS
WHALE

```
S E A H O R S E C J
W A L R U S E A L E
O C T O P U S X A L
R L X S Q U I D M L
D O L P H I N X V Y
F B Z W H A L E X F
I S T I N G R A Y I
S T A R F I S H V S
H E X S H A R K Z H
C R A B T U R T L E
```

Snorkeling is like looking through a window into the ocean. Pretend you're snorkeling. Write about what you see.

_____

_____

_____

_____

_____

_____

_____

_____

_____

_____

_____

_____

_____

_____

_____

_____

_____

_____

Quick Challenges
MAKING THE WORLD A BETTER PLACE

Surprise a friend by making and sharing a list of things you like about them.

_____

_____

_____

_____

Learn about a social issue in your community, such as homelessness, that impacts kids. Write something important that you learn.

_____

_____

_____

_____

Write one thing you can do for a friend who is going through a tough time.

_____

_____

_____

_____

Write down three things you did to help others this week.

_____

_____

_____

_____

Make a wish list. What do you wish could be improved in your community and the world?

_____

_____

_____

_____

In your own words, define the word *kind.* Give an example or two.

_____

_____

_____

_____

With Love from Earth

Think about the gifts our planet gives you. Pick your favorites and write what you love about those gifts.

Imagine This

You come home from school to find a magical box sitting on your doorstep. The box is labeled "Caution: This box has the power to change the world." Write about what happens next.

_____

_____

_____

_____

_____

_____

_____

_____

_____

_____

_____

_____

_____

_____

_____

_____

Admiration Station

Think of a real person you admire who is working to change the world. Perhaps it's a scientist trying to save an endangered species or an engineer helping to keep rivers clean. Write about the work they do.

If you got to interview this person, what would you ask them?

_____

_____

_____

_____

_____

_____

_____

_____

_____

_____

_____

_____

_____

_____

Growing Flowers from Seeds

Which plant grew from which seeds?

Write a story about a squirrel that helps plant trees by burying nuts.

Persuasive Pens

Words can help you convince or persuade others. Think of something you'd like to convince the adults in your life to do, such as organizing a trash pickup day in your neighborhood. Write a letter to them about why this topic is important to you.

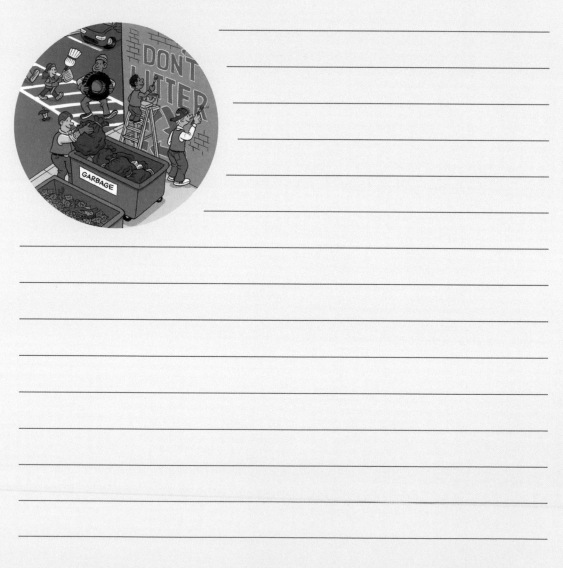

_____

_____

_____

_____

_____

_____

_____

_____

_____

_____

_____

_____

_____

Write about the steps you'd like to take to help improve the situation you've chosen.

_____

_____

_____

_____

_____

_____

_____

_____

_____

_____

Convincing Copy

Persuasive writing:
- Includes facts such as quotes, names, and dates
- Reflects why you care
- Asks the reader to do something like believe in a cause or take action

_____

_____

_____

_____

_____

_____

Make an Infographic!

Images can help readers better understand ideas and words. Think of an endangered species. Use the space here to draw a picture of the animal or plant. Then write facts about the species, connecting them with lines to your image. You just made an infographic!

Infographics

- Blend words and visual images
- Share information in an easy-to-understand way
- Are fun to make (and read!)

Wolves
live in
groups
called
packs.

The New Narwhal

A pod of narwhals has made you an honorary member of the group. You put on a wet suit and jump in the icy water. Write about swimming with narwhals and what you learned about these mysterious creatures.

_____

_____

_____

_____

_____

_____

_____

_____

_____

_____

Create a poster about an animal protection organization that interests you, perhaps one that works to save endangered species or farm animals.

Bike Ride!

Bicycle riding is a fun way to enjoy the great outdoors.
Strap on your helmet and ride your way through this maze.

Imagine your favorite outdoorsy place, such as the beach or the mountains. What is it like to ride your bike through this place?

_____

_____

_____

_____

_____

_____

_____

_____

_____

_____

_____

_____

_____

_____

_____

_____

_____

List three things you love.

_____

_____

_____

Quick Challenges
THINGS YOU LOVE

Think of a friend or family member that you love. What three things do you love about that person?

_____

_____

_____

_____

Describe your dream breakfast.

_____

_____

_____

_____

Imagine your favorite modes of transportation (bicycle? sports car? horse? boat?). Write one sentence each about why they are so great.

_____

_____

_____

_____

What's your favorite sport? What are three things you love about that sport?

_____

_____

_____

_____

What are your three favorite places on Earth?

_____

_____

_____

_____

Pizza Powers

You have been given a magical power for 24 hours: everything you touch turns into pizza. Write about what happens during this delicious day.

Divide up this pizza chart to show how you spent your time on this day with your pizza power.

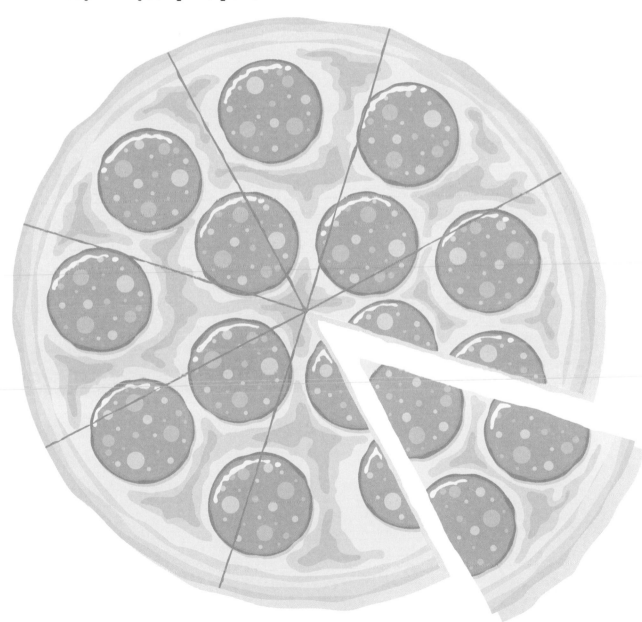

Favorite Athlete

Write about your favorite athlete.

_____

_____

_____

_____

_____

_____

_____

_____

_____

_____

_____

_____

_____

_____

_____

What would you and this athlete talk about if you could hang out together?

Eat Your Veggies

....

You've turned into your favorite vegetable. Write about what happens when a local chef decides they'd like to add you to their soup.

_____

_____

_____

_____

_____

_____

_____

_____

_____

_____

_____

_____

_____

_____

_____

_____

Book Review

These bookworms love to read. They have read all the books on these shelves except for one. Use the clues to figure out which book they haven't read yet.

WALLY AND WENDY HAVE READ

1. All the books with blue covers.
2. All the books about sports.
3. All the books with a person's name in the title.
4. All the books on the middle shelf.

Write a review of your favorite book.

_____

_____

_____

_____

_____

_____

_____

_____

_____

_____

_____

_____

_____

Make Sure to Include:

- The book's title
- The author's name
- A brief summary of the plot
- Comments about what you liked and didn't like

Write a Shape Poem

Pick a favorite thing—such as a giraffe, baseball, or lizard—
and write a short poem or a list of words to describe your topic.

Rearrange the words from your poem into the shape of your topic here.

Coming to Your Senses

The next time you eat your favorite foods, write your observations on this chart. What sounds do you hear when you crunch nachos? How does it feel to eat ice cream or slurp watermelon?

Food	Observations (shape, size, color, texture, smell, sound, taste)

Write a story about a hungry character who gets into trouble while following the scent of their favorite food: french fries.

Painting Pictures with Words

Your five senses—what you see, feel, smell, hear, and taste—provide great details about you and your experiences. Sensory details make your writing specific and clear. For example, the sentence *The dog whined and jumped up and down, shaking the floor* conveys more information than *The dog got excited*.

Recycled Words

Get out some old magazines or newspapers, construction paper, scissors, and glue. Draft a note of encouragement to a friend, neighbor, or family member below. Then, on the next page, rewrite it using a colorful collage of cutout letters and words.

Poetry Slam

Invite your friends and family to a poetry reading. Set a date, and then draft an invitation asking them to write (and share) any kind of poem (or even just a few simple sentences) about something or someone that they love.

Create a list of awards to honor your participants in categories such as the best rhyming words, funniest, or most inspirational.

Blueberry Pickers

Can you find these hidden pictures?

fish

broom

ring

horseshoe

fishhook

sunglasses

bell

sock

bird

mitten

needle

toothbrush

snail

Imagine a conversation between the two kids in the illustration.
What are they talking about?

Check your dictionary for words that begin with the same letter. Write a tongue twister about your favorite (or least favorite) holiday foods using the words you find.

_____

_____

_____

_____

Quick Challenges
CELEBRATIONS

What are some important holidays that your family celebrates each year?

_____

_____

_____

_____

Think of a person you know who has different family traditions than your own and ask about them. Write a couple similarities and differences between their traditions and yours.

_____

_____

_____

_____

Make a list of ultimate party favors, like a leaf blower that shoots confetti or a unicorn mask that grants wishes.

_____

_____

_____

_____

Make a list of seven things, small or large, to celebrate for each day of the coming week.

_____

_____

_____

_____

Brainstorm wild celebrations that animals might have when humans aren't looking. For instance, do bees host honey hoedowns? Do dogs have dance parties?

_____

_____

_____

_____

Nutty National Days

Research national days that celebrate specific things.
Make a list of your favorites here.

Write about why people should celebrate your favorite day—such as National Macadamia Nut Day or Eat Your Beans Day.

_____

_____

_____

_____

_____

_____

_____

_____

_____

_____

_____

_____

_____

_____

_____

_____

_____

_____

Wacky Wednesdays

The president has put you in charge of making Wacky Wednesday a national holiday. Write about how people might celebrate.

_____

_____

_____

_____

_____

_____

_____

_____

_____

_____

_____

_____

_____

_____

_____

_____

As you might have predicted, the first national Wacky Wednesday went off the rails. Write about what happened.

_____

_____

_____

_____

_____

_____

_____

_____

_____

_____

_____

_____

_____

_____

Silly and Spooky

Make up a funny story about an unexpected thing that happened on Halloween.

_____

_____

_____

_____

_____

_____

_____

_____

_____

_____

_____

_____

_____

_____

_____

_____

Write a bedtime story as if you were
reading it to your lovable pet monster.

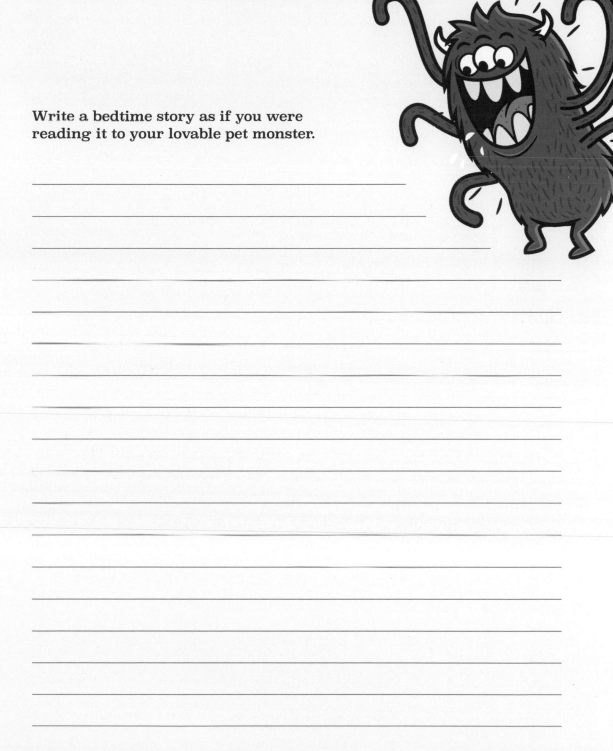

_____

_____

_____

_____

_____

_____

_____

_____

_____

_____

_____

_____

_____

_____

Birthday Party

Someone in your family has a birthday coming up. Write about why you admire them. Make a plan to share it with that person on their birthday.

_____

_____

_____

_____

_____

_____

_____

_____

_____

_____

_____

_____

_____

_____

_____

_____

_____

_____

Write about an epic birthday party you imagine having for this person at a water park.

_____

_____

_____

_____

_____

_____

_____

_____

_____

_____

_____

_____

_____

_____

Family Traditions

Write about family traditions that you love, from your own family or another. What do people eat and do? What do you love most about each tradition?

_____

_____

_____

_____

_____

_____

_____

_____

_____

_____

_____

_____

_____

_____

Invent a silly, new holiday tradition. Describe it here.

_____

_____

_____

_____

_____

_____

_____

_____

_____

_____

_____

_____

_____

_____

_____

Fun Festivities

Family traditions are shared activities, meals, and celebrations passed down from one generation to another. Some are unique or just for fun. Others are related to religious holidays.

Birthday Fun

In the text bubbles, write dialogue for what these characters are saying.

Write a Haiku

Write some haiku about unexpected
holiday guests from a distant galaxy.

_____

_____

_____

_____

_____

_____

_____

_____

_____

_____

_____

_____

Write more haiku about the most
hilarious holiday foods you can imagine.

_____

_____

_____

_____

_____

_____

_____

_____

_____

_____

_____

_____

Tic Tac Row

Each of these cakes has something in common with the other two cakes in the same row. Look at the other rows across, down, and diagonally. Can you tell what's alike in each row?

Pick your favorite cake on the opposite page.
What are some silly ingredients that were put
into this cake? Who was the cake given to?

_____

_____

_____

_____

_____

_____

_____

_____

_____

_____

_____

_____

_____

_____

What are some ways kids will get to school 100 years from now?

_____

_____

_____

_____

You're on your way to vacation on Mars. What are a couple of things you will do there for fun?

_____

_____

_____

_____

You find a strange remote control. When you push the fast-forward button, you're catapulted into the future. Hit pause. What is the first thing you see?

_____

_____

_____

_____

Think of a mistake you made in the past. How will you behave differently in the future based on what you learned?

_____

_____

_____

_____

Start a letter to yourself to read in 10 years.

_____

_____

_____

_____

What are three new things you would like to try in the future?

_____

_____

_____

_____

Chocolate Fountain Trip

You fall headfirst into a huge chocolate fountain. Gasping for air, you wipe the luscious liquid out of your eyes only to realize you've emerged in the same place, but 1,000 years in the future. Write about what happens next.

_____

_____

_____

_____

_____

_____

_____

_____

_____

_____

_____

_____

_____

_____

Create an infographic, such as a diagram or a map,
that provides information about this future place.

Transportation

From horses to helicopters, popular and practical modes of transportation evolve over time. Write about a character who lives 500 years in the future and goes on an exciting and fantastical trip. How do they get there, and what happens along the way?

Our Galaxy

Our galaxy, the Milky Way, is bigger and brighter than most others. Help the astronaut get from start to finish.

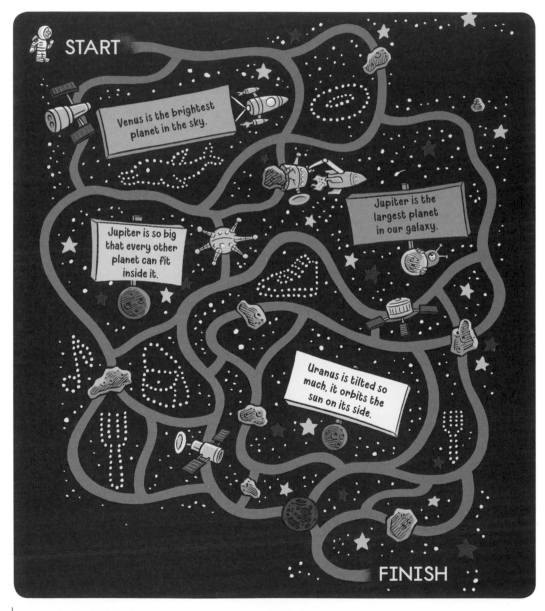

Imagine you're an explorer in the future traveling around the Milky Way. Write a journal entry with details about your most exciting day.

_____

_____

_____

_____

_____

_____

_____

_____

_____

_____

_____

_____

_____

_____

_____

Write Your Autobiography

Pretend it's 20 years in the future. Write about a few moments (real or imagined) of your childhood.

Write about the most important
people in your life.

Auto versus Bio

A writer writes about their own
life in an autobiography. In a
biography, the author writes
about someone else's life story.

Great Expectations

On your birthday, you receive an unexpected letter
in the mail that foretells your future. What does the letter say?

_____

_____

_____

_____

_____

_____

_____

_____

_____

_____

_____

_____

_____

_____

_____

_____

_____

_____

_____

You're excited to read that your future includes traveling to a special and distant place. Describe it here.

_____

_____

_____

_____

_____

_____

_____

_____

_____

_____

_____

_____

_____

_____

Stellar Jigsaw

Which one of these puzzle pieces belongs in the numbered spaces?

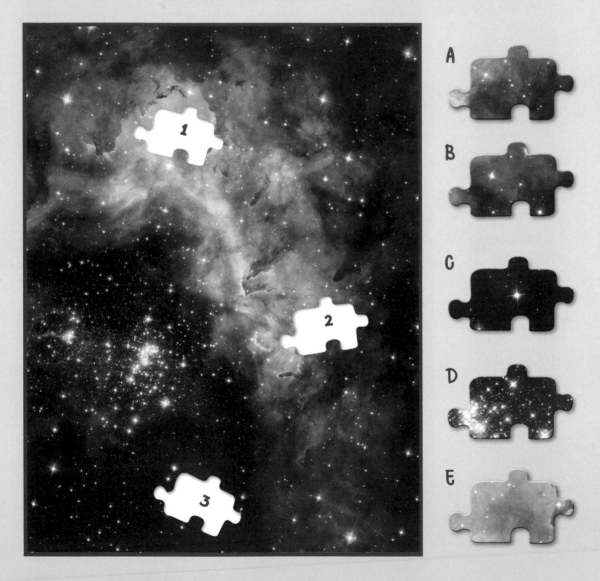

A

B

C

D

E

Bonus! Find where the other puzzle pieces belong.

You're an astronaut on a spacewalk when a fellow astronaut has a dangerous space-suit malfunction. How do you come up with a plan to save the day?

_____

_____

_____

_____

_____

_____

_____

_____

_____

_____

_____

_____

_____

_____

Invention Central

You woke up this morning with a great idea for an invention that will change your life. How does your invention work, and what problems will it solve?

_____

_____

_____

_____

_____

_____

_____

_____

_____

_____

_____

_____

_____

_____

_____

_____

_____

_____

Write about a person in the next century who finds your invention and tries to make sense of it.

ANSWER KEY

BRAVE
pg 23

```
                D   U N A F R A I D
    C O N F I D E N T       E           A
                    T       A     L     D
    S P I R I T E D     N E R V Y   I   V
    P           R   S O L         O   E
    U   I N D O M I T A B L E     N   N
    N K       A   I   E L S       H   T
    K   Y     I   S   A E S       E   U
    Y       I H   H   E D         A   R
            N I   D E F I A N T   D S D O
            T N           A U       S   U
    C O U R A G E O U S   D A U N T L E S S
    H       E     P       T A   R       D
    H E R O I C   P E R S I S T E N T   V A
    K       Y     D     L E O U       I   L
                        U S U D   B O L D
            T E N A C I O U S   A       I
                    K L       R       A T
        G R I T T Y   U N F L I N C H I N G
                    T       N
    H I G H S P I R I T E D     G A M E
```

WELCOME TO CHILLVILLE
pg 64

METAMORPHOSIS
pg 42

OCEAN FIND
pg 84

```
S E A H O R S E C J
W A L R U S E A L E
O C T O P U S X A L
R L X S Q U I D M L
D O L P H I N X V Y
F B Z W H A L E X F
I S T I N G R A Y I
S T A R F I S H V S
H E X S H A R K Z H
C R A B T U R T L E
```

GROWING FLOWERS FROM SEEDS
pg 94

RAINY DAY
pg 50

BIKE RIDE!
pg 102

BOOK REVIEW
pg 112

Wally and Wendy have not yet read
Early Bird Got the Worm!

BLUEBERRY PICKERS
pg 122

TICTACROW
pg 140

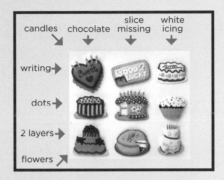

OUR GALAXY
pg 148

STELLAR JIGSAW
pg 154

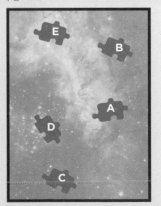

CREDITS

CREDITS

All illustrations by Highlights for Children unless otherwise noted below.
Key: GI=GettyImages, DT=Dreamstime, SS=Shutterstock
6: SasinParaksa/GI; 7: ParkerDeen/GI; 12: FrankRamspott/GI; 13: LokFung/GI (shoe), Mariia Demchenko/GI (notebook); 18: master1305/GI; 22-23: Arseniy Rogov/DT; 25: Sudowoodo/GI (cat); 26: DAMS IMAGE DOLPHINS TK CANNOT FIND IMAGE ORIGIN; 28: KeithBishop/GI; 29: edurivero/GI; 30: Dusan Stankovic/GI; 31: S-S-S/GI; 33: cako74/GI; 35: serazetdinov/GI (megaphone); 37: Galina Shafran/GI; 38: DAMS IMAGE EAGLE TK CANNOT FIND IMAGE ORIGIN, hudiemm/GI (notebook); 39: filo/GI; 40: umesh chandra/GI (card); 41: Gokcemim/GI (blue background), Mega Pixel/SS (pen); 43: Onfokus/GI; 44: rambo182/GI (hamburger); 45: LokFung/GI (spaceship), Vadim Sazhniev/GI (signpost); 47: LokFung/GI; 48: Evgeny Bagautdinov/GI; 49: FrankvandenBergh/GI; 52: gmm2000/GI; Pautova/GI; 60: mathis-works/GI (people), stockcam/GI (notebook); 61: last19/GI; 62: Yevhenii Dubinko/GI; 63: desifoto/GI; 68: FrankRamspott/GI (question mark), stockcam/GI (notebook); 69: bortonia/GI (shoe); 71: Vershinin-M/GI; 72: mishooo/GI; 73: LeeDaniels/GI; 74: Floortje/GI; 78 lmo/GI (flower), Masha Rasputina/GI (bear); 80: rusm/GI; 81: photohampster/GI (leaves), stockcam/GI (notebook); 82: stockcam/GI; 83: Chakkree Chantakad/GI; calvindexter/GI (globe), stockcam/GI (notebook); 89: VIDOK/GI; 90-91: ayagiz/GI (blue wall background); 92: kimberrywood/GI; 97: designer29/GI; 100: beastfromeast/GI; 101: Rockard/GI; 104: Dimitris66/GI (heart), Designer/GI (baby); 105: Olga Prokopeva/GI (globe); 106: DAMS IMAGE PIZZAS TK CANNOT FIND IMAGE ORIGIN; 107: bortonia/GI; 108: AdShooter/GI; 111: lumpynoodles/GI; 114: Nicholas Cope/GI (lizard), GlobalP/GI (giraffe); 116: Boonchuay1970/GI (watermelon), wsmahar/GI (nachos); 117: Inna Tarasenko/GI; 118: skodonnell/GI (glue), Floortje/GI (scissors), crossbrain66/GI (magazines); 119: TARIK KIZILKAYA/GI; 121: Vadim Sazhniev/GI (ribbon); 122: VeenaMari/GI (blueberries); 124: bombuscreative/GI (confetti popper), Designer/GI (cake); 126: mphillips007/GI; 127: Pannonia/GI; 128: damedeeso/GI; 129: artisteer/GI; 132: tbd/GI; 133: exxorian/GI; 135: Dimitris66/GI; 144: GoodLifeStudio/GI; 149: ARTIST ICON OF MILKY WAY ORIGIN UNKNOWN; 157: bombuscreative/GI

Published by Highlights Press
815 Church Street
Honesdale, Pennsylvania 18431
ISBN: 978-1-64472-783-6
Manufactured in Dongguan, Guangdong, China
Mfg. 07/2021
First edition
Visit our website at Highlights.com.
10 9 8 7 6 5 4 3 2 1
Produced by WonderLab Group, LLC
Writer: Paige Towler
Design: Design Superette, Nicole Lazarus
Copyeditor: Molly Reid
Proofreader: Maya Myers